Religion in Human Culture

The Buddhist Tradition

WORLD RELIGIONS CURRICULUM DEVELOPMENT CENTER
MINNEAPOLIS, MINNESOTA

Project Co-Directors: Lee Smith and Wes Bodin
Project Assistants: Joan Voigt and Pat Noyes

Argus Communications
Niles, Illinois 60648

Photo Credits

Cover Photos
Juan V. Cadiz, Jr./CYR COLOR PHOTO AGENCY   lower middle
Jean-Claude LeJeune   middle left, lower left, lower right
W. Swaan/FREE LANCE PHOTOGRAPHERS GUILD   top

Page
VI B. Gallagher/VAN CLEVE, INC.
 4 B. Gallagher/VAN CLEVE, INC.
 6 Wade Nofziger/CYR COLOR PHOTO AGENCY
 9 Bill Weaver/VAN CLEVE, INC.
12 B. S. Oza/TOM STACK & ASSOC.
14 Giorgio Gualco/BRUCE COLEMAN INC.
19 Donald K. Swearer
22 Keith Gunnar/TOM STACK & ASSOC.
23 Marilyn Silverstone/MAGNUM PHOTOS
27 L. L. T. Rhodes/VAN CLEVE, INC.
31 Keith Gunnar/BRUCE COLEMAN INC.
34 Donald K. Swearer
43 Courtesy, Field Museum of Natural History, Chicago
46 Donald K. Swearer
51 Jonathan T. Wright/BRUCE COLEMAN INC.
54 G. D. Plage/BRUCE COLEMAN INC.
59 Peter Schmid/SHOSTAL ASSOCIATES

Acknowledgments

Excerpts from *Buddhism: The Light of Asia* by Kenneth K. S. Ch'en. Copyright © 1968 by Barron's Educational Series, Inc. Reprinted by permission.

Excerpt adapted from Wm. Theodore de Bary et al.: *Sources of Indian Tradition*, Volume I, copyright © 1958 Columbia University Press, pp. 114–15. Reprinted by permission.

Excerpts from *What the Buddha Taught* by Walpola Sri Rahula. Copyright © 1959 by W. Rahula. Second and enlarged edition, © 1974 by W. Rahula. Reprinted by permission of Grove Press, Inc., and Walpola Rahula.

Excerpts from *No God But God* by Del Byron Schneider, copyright © 1969, Augsburg Publishing House. Reprinted by permission.

Excerpt adapted from pp. 117–22 in *The Religions of Man* (hardbound edition) by Huston Smith. Copyright © 1958 by Huston Smith. By permission of Harper & Row, Publishers, Inc.

Excerpt abridged and adapted from pp. 136–39 in *The Religions of Man* (hardbound edition) by Huston Smith. Copyright © 1958 by Huston Smith. By permission of Harper & Row, Publishers, Inc.

Excerpt from *India: A Modern History* by Percival Spear. Copyright © 1961 by the University of Michigan. Reprinted by permission of the University of Michigan Press.

Excerpt from *World of the Buddha* edited by Lucien Stryk. Copyright © 1968 by Lucien Stryk. Reprinted by permission of Doubleday & Company, Inc.

Religion in Human Culture is a Project of St. Louis Park Independent School District #283, Title III/IV (Part C), ESEA, and the Northwest Area Foundation. The opinions and other contents of this book do not necessarily reflect the position or policy of the State of Minnesota, the U.S. Government, St. Louis Park ISD #283, or the Northwest Area Foundation, and no official endorsement should be inferred.

Designed by Gene Tarpey
Map by Homer Grooman

© Copyright Argus Communications 1978.

Argus Communications
7440 Natchez Avenue
Niles, Illinois 60648

International Standard Book Number:
0-89505-007-2

Library of Congress Number:
78-50914

0 9 8 7 6 5 4 3 2

Contents

Note to the Reader

This book is a collection of readings which have been taken from a variety of sources. It is not to be considered or used as a conventional textbook; rather, the readings are intended as a source of data or information on various practices and concepts found in the Buddhist tradition. A study and analysis of this data should increase your understanding not only of Buddhism but of the people who practice this tradition.

To facilitate your reading, a glossary of several terms relevant to Buddhism is provided at the back of this book. As you encounter words you are unfamiliar with, refer to the glossary for their definitions.

The Kanheri Caves are the site of ancient Buddhist temples near Bombay, India.

READING 1
Conditions of the Times—
India about 2500 Years Ago*
PERCIVAL SPEAR

Buddhism was one of several movements which arose in a period of unrest and turmoil from about the year 600 B.C. Three causes may be hazarded for this turmoil: one material, one moral, and one racial. On the material side there was the transition from a pastoral to an agricultural economy. The Indo-Aryan tribes were settling down, becoming tillers of the soil instead of shepherds of flocks. They were developing cities and becoming attached to the soil. Tribal groups were becoming territorial kingdoms. With crop-raising there began to be a surplus production which led to the development of arts and crafts, to exchange in the form of trade and commerce. Such a transition inevitably meant social tension. The merchant or *vaishya* class rose in importance and resented the privileges claimed by the upper two orders. To put it in modern terms, here was a situation which provided material for middle-class discontent with aristocratic privilege and priestly domination. . . .

The second force at work (in what proportions the two combined we cannot say at this distance of time) was a religious and intellectual turmoil comparable with that of contemporary Greece. There was a striving after spiritual truth . . . and much dissatisfaction with the current Brahminical order [Hinduism]. In the thousand years or so since the Indo-Aryans had arrived the

*Adapted from Percival Spear, *India: A Modern History* (Ann Arbor: University of Michigan Press, 1961), pp. 59-60.

Brahmins or hereditary priests (worshipers of Brahma the creator) had seized the leadership of society from the nobles and had already established the most subtle and powerful domination of all, that of the mind. . . . They had developed the doctrine of *karma* or the law of consequences and the complementary doctrine of transmigration of souls from life to life.[1] But the conditions governing the working of these laws were nonmoral and ritualistic. Reliance was placed on *mantras* or spells, on sacrifice, and on priestly ritual. The developing conscience of the age revolted against this mechanistic form of religion. There grew up a longing for *moksha* or freedom or release from rebirth, the conscience demanding something more than ritual and the mind something more than formulae. With these gropings schools of asceticism and moral discipline and schools of philosophy or intellectual understanding developed. From the former came movements like Buddhism, and from the latter the great Hindu schools of philosophy. . . .

Another element should be added to this turmoil. It was the tension between the non-Aryans admitted to the Hindu fold, and the Brahmins. For example, the tribe in the Nepal hills from which the Buddha came is thought to have been of Mongolian stock. The nobles of such groups had little relish for the Brahmin superiority which they found established in the new society. To sum up, we may say that a period of heart-searching and change was introduced by class tension caused by the economic transition and the rise of a mercantile class, by intellectual and spiritual tension caused by the mechanistic character of Brahmin domination, and by race tension caused by the expansion of Hindu society to include non-Aryan groups.

---

[1]The doctrine of transmigration refers to the cycle of rebirths.

READING 2

Approximate Dates of Origin for Eleven of the World's Living Religions*

Hinduism (1500 B.C.)	1500 B.C.
Judaism (1200 B.C.)	1000 B.C.
Zoroastrianism (660 B.C.) Shinto (660 B.C.) Taoism (604 B.C.) Jainism (599 B.C.) Buddhism (560 B.C.) Confucianism (551 B.C.)	500 B.C.
Christianity (4 B.C.)	B.C. A.D.
	A.D. 500
Islam (A.D. 570)	
	A.D. 1000
Sikhism (A.D. 1469)	A.D. 1500
	A.D. 2000

*Based on Robert Ernest Hume, *The World's Living Religions*, rev. ed. (New York: Charles Scribner's Sons, 1959), p. 2.

The Dhamekah stupa in Sarnath, India, built in the fifth to sixth century A.D., contains relics of the Buddha.
It was built over the ruins of a stupa built in the third century B.C.

READING 3
The Way of the Buddha*
DEL BYRON SCHNEIDER

Buddhism, unlike Hinduism, owes its origin to a founder. Siddhartha is the given name and Gautama the family name of a man who is judged by hundreds of millions of people, from Ceylon to Japan, and throughout large sections of the Asian mainland, to have exerted, by his intellectual integrity, moral persuasiveness, and spiritual insight, the most pervasive influence on the thought and life of the human race.

Pious Buddhists reverently avoid his personal name; they refer to him as *Sakya Muni,* a teacher of the Sakyas, for he was born of a minor noble of the Sakya clan. They call him *Tathagata,* or Truth-revealer, but the name by which he is commonly known is Buddha. The term "Buddha" is not a proper name but an honorary title which means "Enlightened One" or "I Am Awake.". . .

"The Buddha" is a confusing term as a description of the founder because there are many Buddhas; anyone who achieves complete enlightenment becomes a Buddha. But the one which millions revere in the East and who is known in the West simply as "Buddha" is Siddhartha Gautama who was born in what is now Nepal near the border of India around 560 B.C. He lived for 80 years, and his life, like that of other founders of religion, has become a profound example to millions of his fellowmen.

*Adapted from Del Byron Schneider, *No God But God* (Minneapolis: Augsburg Publishing House, 1969), pp. 55–68.

GAUTAMA'S EARLY YEARS

Little really is known about Gautama's birth and childhood. His biography has become interwoven with a great mass of Oriental legend with which for centuries Asians have lovingly surrounded it. Stories of wonders such as a miraculous birth, simultaneous conversion of thousands of disciples, previous and future incarnations [existences], and volumes of alleged teachings written centuries after his death make up this story. There is little doubt among scholars, however, that Gautama was a historical person and that the picture of the world in which he moved and the teachings which he advocated can be learned with reasonable accuracy. It is interesting from the comparative point of view to look at the legend that has grown up around Gautama.

A Vietnamese temple painting shows the Buddha as a child.

It is said that on the fifth day after his birth Hindu astrological experts were called in by his father to forecast his future. It was foretold that two careers were open to him, that he would become either a "universal monarch" or the "Buddha Supreme" of the world. Tradition insists that his father wanted his son to become a world-wide ruler, and therefore decided that he should be brought up in the royal tradition. Above all, he should be spared from seeing what has come to be known as the famous legend of "The Four Passing Sights." The soothsayers had predicted that if the child witnessed these four sights, the four signs of what life really is—old age, sickness, death, and a wandering ascetic—he would forever renounce his life of royal pomp and turn his back on the life of a universal monarch for that of a homeless monk.

When Gautama was 16 he was married to a beautiful princess who bore him a son called Rahula. Legend declares that Yasodhara, his wife, was "majestic as a queen of heaven, constant ever, cheerful night and day, full of dignity and exceeding grace." Gautama and his wife lived in luxury; their robes were "made of the finest fabrics from Benares"; day and night a white umbrella was held over them so they would not be troubled " by the cold or heat or straws or dust or dew." Three palaces were built for them, "one for the rains, one for the winter, and one for the summer," and his father had them fitted "with every kind of gratification for the five senses." But it became evident that this bliss was not to last for long, and it was evident that Gautama was destined to become more and more a stranger in his father's household.

THE FOUR PASSING SIGHTS

At 29 years of age Gautama experienced "The Four Passing Sights." According to the story of Gautama's early life, his father had him attended always by young companions. Whenever his son left the palace, his pathway was cleared of all but youths and maidens so that he was kept ignorant of the common fate of men. The tradition is that Gautama also would have grown up ignorant of the other, less attractive companions of life—old age, disease, and death—had not the gods themselves intervened to assume the shapes that would awaken the young prince to his destiny. One day Gautama asked his charioteer to make ready the state carriage and drive to the park.

> Now the young lord saw, as he was driving to the park, an aged man as bent as a roof gable, decrepit, leaning on a staff, tottering as he walked, afflicted and long past his prime. And seeing him, Gautama said: "That man, good charioteer, what has he done that his hair is not like that of other men nor his body?"
> "He is what is called an aged man, my lord."
> "But why is he called aged?"
> "He is called aged, my lord, because he has not much longer to live."
> "But then, good charioteer, am I, too, subject to old age, one who has not got past old age?"
> "You, my lord, and we, too, we all are of a kind to grow old, we have not got past old age."
> "Why then, good charioteer, enough of the park for today. Drive me back hence to my rooms."
> "Yea, my lord," answered the charioteer, and drove him back. And he, going to his rooms, sat brooding, sorrowful and depressed, thinking, "Shame, then, verily be upon this thing called birth, since to one born old age shows itself like that!"[1]

On another day the young prince saw the second sight, that of a desperately sick man who had fallen by the wayside and was being lifted and dressed by his friends. For the first time Gautama knew how physical misery attends man all the days of his life. The young prince came upon the third sight, according to legend, when he saw a great group of people constructing a funeral pyre

[1]E. H. Brewster, *The Life of Gotama The Buddha.* Compiled from the Pali Canon (London: Kegan Paul, Trench, Trubner and Co., Ltd., 1926), p. 15.

for "the corpse of him who had ended his days." This time the prince learned that all men are subject to death, that no one has passed beyond its reach. These three sights robbed him of his peace of mind. His father tried to cheer him up with elaborate entertainment in the form of dancing girls, for he said: "We must not have Gautama declining to rule; we must not have him going forth from the house to the homeless state; we must not let what the Brahmin soothsayers spoke of him come true."

Although his father increased the pleasures and the abundance that surrounded him, Gautama became more and more distraught. His vision of life had changed; he knew now what life really was, and with it came an insatiable hunger to escape from the kind of living to which he was subjected in his father's home. It was the fourth of the "Passing Sights" that showed Gautama the way out of his predicament. As he and his charioteer were driving in the park, a shaven-headed man, a recluse, wearing the yellow robes of a monk, appeared before him. Here was a calm ascetic whose appearance gave witness to the fact that he had found the answers to the riddle of life. Gautama asked him:

> "You, master, what have you done that your head is not as other men's heads, nor your clothes as those of other men?"
>
> "I, my lord, am one who has gone forth."
>
> "What, master, does that mean?"
>
> "It means, my lord, being thorough in the religious life, thorough in the peaceful life, thorough in good actions, thorough in meritorious conduct, thorough in harmlessness, thorough in kindness to all creatures."
>
> "Excellently indeed, master, are you said to have gone forth, since so thorough is your conduct in all those respects."[2]

The words of the monk soothed the young prince's restless heart. He was resolved to leave his father's home to seek that peace of mind and to gain that freedom from old age, disease, and death that he now knew pressed upon all human existence.

The Buddhist scriptures describe in loving detail the lonely struggle of the young prince in deciding to renounce his high place in the world. His father commanded more and more girls "skilled in all manner of dance and song, and beautiful as celestial nymphs" to satisfy every whim of the brooding prince. But his father was fighting a losing battle. The young prince's increasing

[2]Brewster, *op. cit.,* p. 18.

aversion to passion did not allow him to take pleasure in these spectacles. One night, after a whirl of lavish entertainment, the prince fell into a brief slumber.

"And the women exclaiming, 'He for whose sake we should perform has fallen asleep. Of what use is it to weary ourselves any longer?' threw their various instruments on the ground and lay down. And the lamps fed with sweet-smelling oil continued to burn."

The scriptures, as translated from the *Majjhima Nikaya,* . . . tell how the prince then rose and, stepping with inner revulsion over the sleeping women, left forever the room which had become "like a cemetery filled with dead bodies impaled and left to rot."[3] He made his way to his wife's chamber, and there, gazing fondly down on the sleeping mother of his infant son, he bade an unspoken farewell. That night he shaved off his hair and beard, exchanged his rich garments for the coarse yellow robe of a monk, and walked into the forest to become part of that great anonymous group of monks vowed to live the religious life.

THE WANDERING SEEKER

Gautama was obsessed with the idea of religion—which lies so close to the mind of every Indian—and was willing to face the rigorous discipline necessary for gaining the religious end. He left the land of his native Sakyas and went to Rajagaha, the capital of the neighboring kingdom of Magadha which extended along the Ganges valley. He wandered from place to place in search of a teacher who would guide him to his goal. He first became the disciple of two Hindu masters who were trained in *raja yoga,*[4] and who instructed him in their own doctrine and discipline. But he did not find their techniques compatible to his nature, and he became convinced that the substance of Hinduism or Brahmanism would not conduct him to true enlightenment. There was another way open to him; this was the extreme bodily asceticism which some were then advocating.

He began a series of fasts, engaged in exhaustive exercises of meditation, and inflicted on himself austerities of the worst kind. He came to realize that as "fire cannot be produced from damp

A Thai sculpture depicts the fasting Buddha.

[3]John B. Noss, *Man's Religions* (New York: The Macmillan Company, 1956), pp. 156–58.
[4]A form of yoga that progresses through eight stages, leading to self-realization and liberation.

but dry wood only," those whose passions are not calmed cannot attain enlightenment. If it was his body that was holding him back, he was determined not to allow one sinew to stand in the way. He abandoned food and became a mere skeleton. According to the records of his life, "with gritted teeth and tongue cleaving to my palate I mastered, crushed, and forced my thought by the mind until the sweat oozed out of my armpits." He sat on a bed of thorns, dressed in a hairshirt and other irritating garments, and let the dirt accumulate on his body until it dropped off of its own accord. He reduced his diet to "one or two beans a day" and became exceedingly thin. The records say:

> Like dried cane now became my arms and legs, withered by this extremely scanty diet; like the foot of a camel became my buttock; like a string of beads became my spinal column, with the vertabrae protruding through; just as the roofbeams of an old house sharply protrude, so protruded my ribs; just as in a deep well the little water-stars far beneath are scarcely seen, so now in my eye-balls the sunken pupils are scarcely seen; as a wild gourd, freshly cut, in the hot sun becomes empty and withered, so now became empty and withered the skin of my head. . . . And when I wished to touch my belly, I reached the back of my spine, and when I wished to touch my spine, I again reached to the belly.[5]

GAUTAMA'S ENLIGHTENMENT

Self-denial and severe asceticism did not lead Gautama to the spiritual insights he desired. Though he often found himself at death's door, he was no closer to the riddle of life than when he first started. "Six years of search along the two most widely recognized roads to salvation known to India, philosophic meditation and bodily asceticism, had yielded no results."[6] Finally, having decided that asceticism was not the way to enlightenment, the record of his early life shows that he remembered how once in his youth, "sitting under the shade of a rose-apple tree, aloof from desire, aloof from things not good," he had an experience of mystic contemplation. He wondered now whether this might not be the path which would lead him to the highest wisdom.

Thus it was that in his 35th year in a full-moon evening in May

[5]Brewster, *op. cit.*, pp. 35, 36.
[6]Noss, *op. cit.*, p. 161.

he seated himself at the foot of a tree, which has since come to be known as the *bodhi* tree (meaning "enlightenment"), situated near Gaya in northeast India. Here he entered upon a process of contemplation and meditation that brought him to the climax of his inner struggle. Having seated himself firmly, cross-legged, he made a solemn and historical resolution that was to lead to his enlightenment and to a change of thinking in the lives of millions of people. According to the *Majjhima Nikaya,* he resolved: "Let my skin and sinews and bones become dry . . . and let all the flesh and blood in my body dry up, but never from this seat will I stir, until I have attained the supreme and absolute wisdom."

At this point tradition has recorded a great temptation scene. Mara, the Evil One, "the bringer of death and the enemy of truth," realizing that Gautama was about to pass beyond his control, rushed his evil forces to the *bodhi* tree to disrupt his concentrations. The Tempter, with his three daughters, Tanha, Raga, and Arati, and his host of evil demons sought to kindle desire in the heart of the Buddha-to-be. In one of the temptations, the Tempter disguised himself as Death. The personification of evil and his powerful hosts attacked Gautama with great thunderstorms, showers of rocks, and live coals that came smoking and flaming and crashing through the air, followed, finally, by a great darkness. But because of the strength of his perfections from previous births, Gautama remained unmoved; the flames of hell became wholesome breezes of perfume, and the angry thunderbolts were changed into lotus blossoms.

In one final, desperate act the Evil One challenged Gautama's right to be doing what he was doing, to be piercing, as it were, the very secrets of the universe. Thereupon, drawing forth his right hand from beneath his robes, the Buddha-to-be stretched it out toward the mighty earth and said, "Are you witness, or are you not . . . ?" And the mighty earth thundered, "I bear you witness!" with a hundred, a thousand, a hundred thousand roars, as if to overwhelm the army of Mara. While Mara's army was put to flight, the host of the gods descended from heaven and made offerings of garlands, perfumes, and ointments, and in many a hymn extolled the victor. While the *bodhi* tree, in homage, rained "red coral-like sprigs upon his priestly robes" that fateful night in May, and while Gautama's mind was at last piercing the bubble of the universe, the record says that the earth quaked 12 times, lotuses bloomed on every tree, fruit trees were weighted down by their burden of fruit, and the whole earth became like a bouquet of flowers while the oceans became sweet to the taste and the rivers checked their flowing. For 49 days he stayed under the *bodhi* tree, deep in rapture, after which his "glorious glance" opened again onto the world with its remedy for the ills of mankind. With this triumph a new chapter opened in the history of man's spiritual achievement.

However, the Buddha was confronted with a temptation far more insidious than the direct assaults of the Tempter. The scriptures state that he was besought by the Evil One to keep this newly-won truth to himself. After all, who could be expected to understand such truth? Men would misunderstand him, for they would not be able to comprehend "what goes against the stream, abstruse, deep, difficult to perceive, and subtle." Would it not be better to keep to himself what he obtained through so much effort? Why not simply enter the blessed state of the hereafter or *Nirvana* and be done with the world forever? In one of the best-attested facts in the record of the Buddha's life,[7] we are told that this temptation was real to him—the temptation to pass away without attempting to proclaim to others the glad tidings of the noble way. But after intense mental struggle he began his preaching ministry declaring that "there will be some that will understand the *dharma* (the truth)."

Bodhi tree sculpture in Sanchi, where the best preserved Buddhist monuments in India are found.

The Buddha adopted a mendicant [dependent on alms] missionary's life with its poverty, unpopularity, and opposition. He did not merely preach, but he lived the kind of life which he taught other men to live. He is reported to have preached his first sermon in the Deer Park in Benares in northern India. He urged his disciples to avoid the two extremes of sensual pleasure and self-denial and to follow the middle course. Inspired by his preaching, thousands came forward to become resident members of the Buddhist monastic order called the *Sangha*. The rules for admittance into the order were few: the wearing of the yellow robe, the adoption of the shaven head, the carrying of the begging bowl, and the habit of daily meditation. Every initiate subscribed to the confession: "I take refuge in the Buddha, I take refuge in the Teaching (*Dharma*). I take refuge in the Order (*Sangha*)."

. . . From the very beginning monks were encouraged by Buddha to undertake the work of missions, for in the words which

[7]See T. W. Rhys Davids, *Buddhism: Its History and Literature* (New York: G. P. Putnam's Sons, 3rd edition), pp. 104–105.

have now become famous Buddha said: "Go forth, mendicant brothers, upon journeys for the help of the many, for the well-being of the many, out of compassion for the world . . . for the well-being of spirits and men."[8]

For a while Buddhism became the dominant religion of India and, under King Asoka in the third century B.C., trained missionaries were sent out to spread the teaching in all directions. This continued until the subsequent eclipse of Buddhism in India and the development of Theravada Buddhism in southern Asia.

For 45 years the Buddha himself traveled far and wide, and the number of his disciples increased with each passing year. "Brahmins and monks, hermits and outcasts, noble ladies and repentant sinners" joined the community. About 480 B.C., when the Buddha was 80 years old and on one of his preaching trips, he journeyed to an obscure town by the name of Kusinara, northeast of Benares. Before leaving on the slow three-month journey, he had predicted to Ananda, his cousin and favorite disciple, that his time had come to enter *Nirvana,* that place where his earthly existence would come to an end. According to the traditional story of his life, while dining one day at the home of Cunda, a goldsmith, he came down with severe dysentery, evidently caused by some poisoned food. Despite his critical condition, he continued toward Kusinara, but when he could journey no more, he lay down under the shady bough of a tree. His last words to his disciples were:

> "My age is now full ripe, my life draws to a close:
> I leave you, I depart, relying on myself alone!
> Be earnest then, O brethren, holy, full of thought!
> Be steadfast in resolve! Keep watch o'er your own hearts!
> Who wearies not, but holds fast to his truth and law,
> Shall cross this sea of life, shall make an end of grief."[9]

---

[8] Joseph Kitagawa, *Religions of the East* (Philadelphia: The Westminster Press, 1960), p. 160.
[9] E. A. Burtt, *The Teachings of the Compassionate Buddha* (New York: The New American Library, 1955), p. 50.

Woman in Sri Lanka prays before the Buddha's statue. Following the Noble Eightfold Path leads Buddhists to happiness and peace through moral, spiritual, and intellectual perfection.

READING 4
The Fourth Noble Truth:
Magga: 'The Path'
WALPOLA SRI RAHULA

The Buddha set forth his convictions about life in what is known as the Four Noble Truths. These may be summarized as (1) all life is dukkha *(suffering), (2) this suffering is caused by selfish desire or craving, (3) it is possible to destroy this craving, (4) this craving and the suffering that it causes can be overcome by following the Noble Eightfold Path. The steps in this Eightfold Path are the subject of the following reading.*

The Fourth Noble Truth is that of the Way leading to the Cessation of *Dukkha* [suffering]. This is known as the 'Middle Path' because it avoids two extremes: one extreme being the search for happiness through the pleasures of the senses, which is 'low, common, unprofitable and the way of the ordinary people'; the other being the search for happiness through . . . different forms of asceticism, which is 'painful, unworthy and unprofitable'. Having himself first tried these two extremes, and having found them to be useless, the Buddha discovered through personal experience the Middle Path 'which gives vision and knowledge, which leads to Calm, Insight, Enlightenment, Nirvana'. This Middle Path is generally referred to as the Noble Eightfold Path, because it is composed of eight categories or divisions: namely,

*From Walpola Sri Rahula, *What the Buddha Taught,* rev. ed. (New York: Grove Press, 1974), pp. 45–50.

1. Right Understanding,
2. Right Thought,
3. Right Speech,
4. Right Action,
5. Right Livelihood,
6. Right Effort,
7. Right Mindfulness,
8. Right Concentration.

Practically the whole teaching of the Buddha, to which he devoted himself during 45 years, deals in some way or other with this Path. He explained it in different ways and in different words to different people, according to the stage of their development and their capacity to understand and follow him. But the essence of those many thousand discourses scattered in the Buddhist Scriptures is found in the Noble Eightfold Path.

It should not be thought that the eight categories or divisions of the Path should be followed and practised one after the other in the numerical order as given in the usual list above. But they are to be developed more or less simultaneously, as far as possible according to the capacity of each individual. They are all linked together and each helps the cultivation of the others.

These eight factors aim at promoting and perfecting the three essentials of Buddhist training and discipline: namely: (a) Ethical Conduct, (b) Mental Discipline and (c) Wisdom. It will therefore be more helpful for a coherent and better understanding of the eight divisions of the Path, if we group them and explain them according to these three heads.

Ethical Conduct is built on the vast conception of universal love and compassion for all living beings, on which the Buddha's teaching is based. It is regrettable that many scholars forget this great ideal of the Buddha's teaching, and indulge in only dry philosophical and metaphysical divagations [digressions] when they talk and write about Buddhism. The Buddha gave his teaching 'for the good of the many, for the happiness of the many, out of compassion for the world'.

According to Buddhism, for a man to be perfect there are two qualities that he should develop equally: compassion on one side, and wisdom on the other. Here compassion represents love, charity, kindness, tolerance and such noble qualities on the emotional side, or qualities of the heart, while wisdom would stand for the intellectual side or the qualities of the mind. If one develops only the emotional neglecting the intellectual, one may become a good-hearted fool; while to develop only the intellectual side neglecting the emotional may turn one into a hard-hearted intellect without feeling for others. Therefore, to be perfect one has to develop both equally. That is the aim of the Buddhist way of life: in it wisdom and compassion are inseparably linked together. . . .

Now, in Ethical Conduct, based on love and compassion, are included three factors of the Noble Eightfold Path: namely, Right Speech, Right Action and Right Livelihood. (Nos. 3, 4 and 5 in the list).

Right speech means abstention (1) from telling lies, (2) from . . . slander and talk that may bring about hatred, enmity [ill-will], disunity and disharmony among individuals or groups of people, (3) from harsh, rude, impolite, malicious and abusive language, and (4) from idle, useless and foolish babble and gossip. When one abstains from these forms of wrong and harmful speech one naturally has to speak the truth, has to use words that are friendly and benevolent, pleasant and gentle, meaningful and useful. One should not speak carelessly: speech should be at the right time and place. If one cannot say something useful, one should keep 'noble silence'.

Right Action aims at promoting moral, honourable and peaceful conduct. It admonishes us that we should abstain from destroying life, from stealing, from dishonest dealings, from illegitimate sexual intercourse, and that we should also help others to lead a peaceful and honourable life in the right way.

Right Livelihood means that one should abstain from making one's living through a profession that brings harm to others, such as trading in arms and lethal weapons, intoxicating drinks, poisons, killing animals, cheating, etc., and should live by a profession which is honourable . . . and innocent of harm to others. One can clearly see here that Buddhism is strongly opposed to any kind of war, when it lays down that trade in arms and lethal weapons is an evil and unjust means of livelihood.

These three factors (Right Speech, Right Action and Right Livelihood) of the Eightfold Path constitute Ethical Conduct. It should be realized that the Buddhist ethical and moral conduct aims at promoting a happy and harmonious life both for the individual and for society . This moral conduct is considered as the indispensable foundation for all higher spiritual attainments. No spiritual development is possible without this moral basis.

Next comes Mental Discipline, in which are included three other factors of the Eightfold Path: namely, Right Effort, Right Mindfulness (or Attentiveness) and Right Concentration. (Nos. 6, 7 and 8 in the list).

Right Effort is the energetic will (1) to prevent evil and unwholesome states of mind from arising, and (2) to get rid of such evil and unwholesome states that have already arisen within a man, and also (3) to produce . . . good and wholesome states of mind not yet arisen, and (4) to develop and bring to perfection the good and wholesome states of mind already present in man.

Right Mindfulness (or Attentiveness) is to be diligently aware, mindful and attentive with regard to (1) the activities of the body, (2) sensations or feelings, (3) the activities of the mind and (4) ideas, thoughts, conceptions and things.

The practice of concentration on breathing is one of the well-known exercises, connected with the body, for mental development. There are several other ways of developing attentiveness in relation to the body—as modes of meditation.

With regard to sensations and feelings, one should be clearly aware of all forms of feelings and sensations, pleasant, unpleasant and neutral, of how they appear and disappear within oneself.

Concerning the activities of mind, one should be aware whether one's mind is lustful or not, given to hatred or not, . . . distracted or concentrated, etc. In this way one should be aware of all movements of mind, how they arise and disappear.

As regards ideas, thoughts, conceptions and things, one should know their nature, how they appear and disappear, how they are developed, how they are suppressed, and destroyed, and so on. . . .

The third and last factor of Mental Discipline is Right Concentration leading to the four stages of *Dhyana,* generally called trance. . . . In the first stage of *Dhyana,* passionate desires and certain unwholesome thoughts like sensuous lust, ill-will, . . . worry, restlessness, and skeptical doubt are discarded, and feelings of joy and happiness are maintained, along with certain mental activities. In the second stage, all intellectual activities are suppressed, tranquillity and 'one-pointedness' of mind [deep concentration] developed, and the feelings of joy and happiness are still retained. In the third stage, the feeling of joy, which is an active sensation, also disappears, while the disposition of happiness still remains in addition to mindful equanimity [a sense of calmness]. In the fourth stage of *Dhyana,* all sensations, even of happiness and unhappiness, of joy and sorrow, disappear, only pure equanimity and awareness remaining.

Thus the mind is trained and disciplined and developed through Right Effort, Right Mindfulness, and Right Concentration.

The remaining two factors, namely Right Thought and Right Understanding, . . . constitute Wisdom.

Right Thought denotes the thoughts of selfless renunciation or detachment, thoughts of love and thoughts of non-violence, which are extended to all beings. It is very interesting and important to note here that thoughts of selfless detachment, love and non-violence are grouped on the side of wisdom. This clearly shows that true wisdom is endowed with these noble qualities, and that all thoughts of selfish desire, ill-will, hatred and violence are the result of a lack of wisdom—in all spheres of life whether individual, social, or political.

Right Understanding is the understanding of things as they are, and it is the Four Noble Truths that explain things as they really are. Right Understanding therefore is ultimately reduced to the understanding of the Four Noble Truths. This understanding is the highest wisdom which sees the Ultimate Reality. According to Buddhism there are two sorts of understanding: What we generally call understanding is knowledge, an accumulated memory, an intellectual grasping of a subject according to certain given data. This is called 'knowing accordingly'. It is not very deep. Real deep understanding is called 'penetration', seeing a thing in its true nature, without name and label. This penetration is possible only when the mind is free from all impurities and is fully developed through meditation.

From this brief account of the Path, one may see that it is a way of life to be followed, practised and developed by each individual. It is self-discipline in body, word and mind, self-development and self-purification. It has nothing to do with belief, prayer, worship or ceremony. In that sense, it has nothing which may popularly be called 'religious'. It is a Path leading to the realization of Ultimate Reality, to complete freedom, happiness and peace through moral, spiritual and intellectual perfection.

A monk in a forest hermitage meditates in order to gain mental discipline.

In Buddhist countries there are simple and beautiful customs and ceremonies on religious occasions. They have little to do with the real Path. But they have their value in satisfying certain religious emotions and the needs of those who are less advanced, and helping them gradually along the Path.

With regard to the Four Noble Truths we have four functions to perform:

The First Noble Truth is *Dukkha,* the nature of life, its suffering, its sorrows and joys, its imperfection and unsatisfactoriness, its impermanence and insubstantiality [lack of substance]. With regard to this, our function is to understand it as a fact, clearly and completely.

The Second Noble Truth is the Origin of *Dukkha,* which is desire, 'thirst', accompanied by all other passions. . . . A mere understanding of this fact is not sufficient. Here our function is to discard it, . . . to destroy and eradicate it.

The Third Noble Truth is the Cessation of *Dukkha,* Nirvana, the Absolute Truth, the Ultimate Reality. Here our function is to realize it.

The Fourth Noble Truth is the Path leading to the realization of Nirvana. A mere knowledge of the Path, however complete, will not do. In this case, our function is to follow it and keep to it.

READING 5
The Teachings of the Buddha*
KENNETH K. S. CH'EN

As in the case of the other two great teachers who were roughly contemporaneous with the Buddha—Socrates and Confucius—no records were kept of the teachings of the master while he lived. He merely traveled from place to place preaching the doctrines orally to all those who came to listen, while his disciples also transmitted them orally after having memorized them. We do not know exactly just when and where the teachings were first reduced to writing. In the middle of the third century B.C., the Indian monarch Asoka issued an edict calling upon his subjects to abide by the teachings of the Blessed One, and suggested certain titles of discourses which they should study. This might suggest that there were written texts at the time, but this is by no means certain. The only sure thing is that the earliest written compilation of the Buddhist scriptures was made in Pali (an Indian literary language) during the first century B.C., and it is on the basis of this Pali canon that we shall now base our discussion of the Buddha's teachings. We use the term Hinayana or the Lesser Vehicle to designate these teachings, but a more appropriate term would be Theravada, or Doctrine of the Elders. In our discussion we shall on occasion use the Pali word dhamma to refer to these teachings of the Buddha. The Sanskrit spelling of

*Slightly adapted from Kenneth K. S. Ch'en, *Buddhism: The Light of Asia,* (Woodbury, N. Y.: Barron's Educational Series, 1968), pp. 30–33, 44–46.

the word is dharma. The Sanskrit spelling will be used whenever Mahayan Buddhism and Sanskrit literature are involved.

The Buddha often said that he offered his teachings in the manner of a physician, who had diagnosed the condition of the patient and then prescribed the method of cure. The therapy had worked in his case, and he assured his listeners that it would work in others also, if only they would follow the course of action he prescribed. In following his therapy of an arduous self-ordained discipline, there was to be no recourse to the supernatural for assistance. Very often he characterized his discipline as being that of the middle path. He steered a course that avoided the pursuit of austerities and self-torture on the one hand and the pursuit of sensual pleasures on the other. Another set of extremes that the Buddha avoided consisted of nihilism, everything is not, and materialism, everything is; instead he stressed that every-thing is a becoming. The goal of the therapy is the cessation of the ceaseless rounds of rebirths. The way to do this is to extinguish the fires of lust and desire that generate karma and kept the individual hankering for continued existence.

This stone, found in a Burmese temple, is inscribed with the teachings of the Buddha.

The word karma means deed. The doctrines of karma and rebirth [samsara] were already present in India before the Buddha was born, and when he formulated his system, he incorporated them into it. The doctrine of karma provides an explanation for the diversity of living beings, for good deeds are rewarded and evil deeds punished automatically, with no room for a mystical or theological agency to intervene. As a result of the deeds performed in the past or present, a living being would continue in the cycle of rebirth and assume a different form in each rebirth. To the Indians, therefore, life is usually symbolized by a circle, the circle of life with no beginning and no end. The aim of Buddhism as with all Indian religions is to break this circle at some point, so that the living being no longer continues to transmigrate. Once this is achieved, the individual is said to have achieved emancipation. Since the form of each successive rebirth is determined by karma, the greatest importance is attached to it.

The Buddha accepted the prevailing views concerning karma, but also added a significant point. He taught that not only the deed but also the intention or will behind the deed is important, and that karma is generated only when intention is present. Here we see why in his system the Buddha attached so much impor-

A stupa and ruins of a monastery mark the site at Sarnath where the Buddha gave his first sermon.

tance to the discipline of the mind. The Buddhist definition of karma is intention or will plus bodily action. Every thought or act leaves behind some traces which could not be erased. Now this definition has a bearing on the Buddhist confession, which does not remove the sin of wrongdoing but merely is a repentance or affirmation that the doer would not repeat the offensive act. The traces of karma would be manifested in the present existence, or in future existences. Thus a living being, after performing some evil deeds in his present life, would require numerous lives in the future to work out the consequences of that act, and some of the consequences might be rebirth in a lower form of existence.

In the Buddhist scheme of life, there are five states of existences: deity, man, animal, hungry ghost, and resident of hell. A hungry ghost is described as a creature continually tormented by hunger because he has a head the size of a pin-head sitting on top of a huge belly. The first two are considered to be honorable states; the last three, evil. Rebirth as a deity is not everlasting, however, for the deities are still subject to karma. Once the fruits of honorable karma have been exhausted, the deities will fall from their high state and be reborn in a lower one. Rebirth as a man is considered the most desirable, because it is only man who can achieve salvation and nirvana. However, to be reborn as a man is extremely difficult, as illustrated by a favorite simile of the Buddhists. Imagine a limitless expanse of the ocean, on which a tile is floating, with a hole in it just large enough for a turtle's head to go through. Now imagine also a turtle which comes up to the surface of the ocean just once in a century. How difficult it is indeed for that turtle to come up just at the right time and the right place to put his head into the hole in the tile floating aimlessly about. Yet the Buddhists say it is easier for the turtle to do so than it is to attain rebirth as a man.

If, as the Buddhists say, we are what we are through the operation of karma, is there any room for will or intention? Would not our intention and will also be predetermined? To these questions the Buddhists give no definite answer. They only teach that we are not only the heirs to our previous existences, but also the creators of our future, for the doctrine of karma leaves room for personal will and action. Through the operation of karma, man need not look outside himself for assistance to reach the goal of the religious life. Only he can save himself, only he can walk the path that the Buddha had pointed out. Because of this emphasis, the Buddhist would do away with all distinctions of peoples based on birth or caste or wealth. No matter what one may be, he is just as privileged as any other to join the monastic community and strive for the highest goal of religious life.

Another important Buddhist doctrine is that of anatta, *or the doctrine that there is no permanent self or soul. This doctrine is discussed in another excerpt from Kenneth Ch'en's* Buddhism: The Light of Asia.

It was already taught in the Upanishads [early Hindu sacred writing] that the individual self is the same as the universal self, and that as soon as one realizes this identity, he is liberated. Consequently, for followers of the Upanishads, the greatest object of attachment is this individual self, as evidenced by the following passage, "That self is dearer than a son, is dearer than wealth, is dearer than all else. One should reverence the self alone as dear. He who reverences the self alone as dear, what he holds dear, verily, is not perishable."[1] To the brahman, therefore, the individual self is his soul, which enters the material body at birth and leaves it at death. As it is immaterial and invisible, it remains the same amidst all the different states of existences that a living being undergoes. Its existence insures to each individual the fruits of his actions and thoughts, so that he may reap his rewards in immortality or punishment in hell.

The Buddha held that this belief in a permanent self or soul is one of the most deceitful delusions ever held by man, for it gives rise to attachment, attachment to egoism, egoism to cravings for pleasure and fame, which in turn led to suffering. In order to draw people away from this attachment to the self, the Buddha boldly denied its existence, hoping that by knocking down the main prop of the Upanishadic teachings, he would be able to gain a hearing for his ideas. He held that this false belief in a permanent self is due to an erroneous conception of a unity behind the elements that comprise the individual. He said that he had searched everywhere for this permanent self or soul, but found only a mixture of the five *skandhas* or aggregates: material body, feelings, perception, predispositions, and consciousness. At any one moment, according to him, we are but a temporary composition

[1]R. A. E. Hume, *The Thirteen Principal Upanishads* (London: Oxford University Press, 1931), p. 83.

of the five aggregates, and as these change every moment, so does the composition. Therefore all that we are is but a continuous living entity which does not remain the same for any two consecutive moments, but which comes into being and disappears as soon as it arises. Why then should we attach so much importance to this transitory entity, in which there is no permanent self or soul? Once we accept this truth of the non-existence of a permanent self, when we see that what we call the self is nothing but a stream of perishing physical and mental phenomena, then we destroy our selfish desires and self-interests, and instead of suffering from anxieties and disappointments, we will enjoy peace of mind and tranquility.

If there is no permanent self or soul but only a temporary combination of the five aggregates, then what is it that suffers rebirth in the different states of existence? What is it that stores up karma and then expends it? Wouldn't the doctrine of non-self mean that there is no relation between a living being and his acts, for who is there to receive the fruits of acts done in the past and eventually enter nirvana? In answer to this problem, Buddhism furnishes the following answer. When a living being dies, the five aggregates that constitute the living being disintegrate, but because of the karma accrued in the past, there must be fulfillment, and so there is rebirth. The Buddhist belief in the regularity of the operation of karma is so strong that there can be no interference with its operation. The force of past karma causes a new being to come into existence, a new collection of the five aggregates, which inherits the fruits of the past karma and whose form is determined by those fruits. However, the Buddhists also explain that while this new complex which is reborn is not the same as the one just passed away, it is not different either, for a living being is not merely a combination of the five aggregates but is also a series of states, originating in dependence one upon the other, and continuing through endless numbers of existences. As one writer puts it, it is a continuity of an ever changing entity; there is continuity but there is no sameness, just as a flame is not the same nor a different flame.

Numerous similes are found in the Buddhist literature to illustrate this idea. The favorite is the river of life. A river "maintains one constant form, one seeming entity, though not one single drop remains today of all the volume that composed the river yesterday."[2] A living being is like that river. Another favorite is that of the candle. If we light one candle with another, the transmitted flame is one and the same, for there is no interruption of the flame, but the two candles are not the same. Similarly there is continuity in the operation of karma, even though the two collections of aggregates are not the same. In further illustration of this point, the Buddha told the following story. A man bought some milk, and then said he would return the following day to get it. When he returned, the milk had turned into curd. The man said he had bought milk, not curd, but the milkman retorted it was milk yesterday, but curd today. In order to settle the dispute, the Buddha was consulted, and he decided in favor of the milkman, for, as he said, the curd sprang from the milk, and it was the same stream of development. To the Buddhist, therefore, the history of an individual does not begin at birth, but reaches back to countless rebirths in the past, and to the countless lives in the past that at one time or another had touched upon that individual stream.

The Buddhist doctrine of *anatta* or no-self may therefore be stated in the following terms. There is no self, no soul. There is only a living complex of mental and physical elements succeeding one another continuously, living on the fruits of its acts. Because of this, it can control itself, and can exert efforts to better itself, so that by the proper discipline, it is able to attain nirvana or deliverance. In nirvana, this living composite dissolves to be reborn no more, for there is no more karma to bring about a rebirth.

[2]S. Z. Aung, *Compendium of Philosophy* (London: Luzac, 1956), Introduction, p. 9.

READING 6
The End of Life—Nirvana*
DEL BYRON SCHNEIDER

The serene face of the Golden Buddha in Bangkok, Thailand.

Just what *Nirvana,* or the final state of man, will be, Buddha did not explain. The word means "blown out" . . . or "extinct." It might appear that . . . *Nirvana* is annihilation. Buddha did not say that. He did not know whether that was true or not. All he cared to know was that *Nirvana* was the final peace, the eternal state of being. His disciples had seen in the Buddha a reality which they wanted in their own lives. Their testimony is that progress along the path which Buddha advocated brings an enlargement to human life as well as the hope of eternal bliss. But how to describe for his followers the state in which all identification with a man's historical, finite self is obliterated while experience itself remains and is magnified beyond all imagination, did not occupy the mind of the Buddha. The path itself, not the goal, was the important consideration. When he was asked by a wandering monk if it was possible to illustrate by a simile the place called *Nirvana,* the Buddha replied:

"If a fire were blazing in front of you, would you know what it was?"
"Yes, good Gotama."
"And would you know if it were to be put out?"
"Yes, good Gotama."
"And on its being put out, would you know the direction the fire

*From Schneider, *No God But God,* pp. 77–79.

had gone to from here—east, west, north, south?"
"This question does not apply, good Gotama."

The Buddha then closed the discussion by pointing out that the question the ascetic had asked about existence after death was not rightly put, either. "Feelings, perceptions, those impulses, that consciousness" by which one defines a human being have passed away from him who has attained *Nirvana*. "He is deep, immeasurable, unfathomable, as is the great ocean."[1]

[1]E. A. Burtt, *The Teachings of the Compassionate Buddha* (New York: The New American Library, 1955), pp. 115–16.

READING 7
The Way Out of the World*

The following selection is from The Questions of King Milinda, *written by an unknown author in northern India around the first or second century* A.D. *The text, written in the form of dialogues, answers many questions on Buddhist doctrine. Its greatest influence was felt not in India, however, but in Ceylon (now Sri Lanka) and the countries of Southeast Asia.*

The conversations recorded in this book probably never took place. The questions are attributed to King Milinda, or Menander, a Greek ruler of a large empire in northwestern India in the late second century B.C. *He was one of the greatest of the Indo-Greek kings and is believed to have been a patron of Buddhism. The answers in these dialogues are provided by Nagasena, an esteemed monk.*

Milinda-panha (*The Questions of King Milinda*), ed. V. Trenck-ner, (London: William and Norgate, 1880), pp. 313-26.

"Venerable one, is nirvana all bliss, or is it mixed with suffering?"

"Nirvana is entirely bliss, Great King, and there is no suffering in it."

"We cannot believe that nirvana is all bliss; we maintain that it is mixed with suffering. For we can see that those who seek

*From Stephan Beyer, *The Buddhist Experience: Sources and Interpretations,* The Religious Life of Man Series (Encino, Calif.: Dickenson Publishing Co., 1974), pp. 200-206.

nirvana torment their bodies and their minds: they restrain their standing and walking and sitting and eating; they interrupt their sleep; they oppress their senses; and they cast aside their wealth and friends and kinsmen.

"But those who are happy and full of bliss in the world delight their senses with pleasure. They delight their eyes with all manner of beautiful sights, and their ears with all manner of music and song; they delight their nose with the scent of fruits and flowers and fragrant plants, and their tongue with the sweet taste of food and drink. They delight their body with the touch of the soft and fine, the tender and the delicate; and they delight their mind with thoughts and ideas both virtuous and sinful, both good and bad. And they do these things whenever they like.

"But you do not develop your senses; you slay and destroy and hinder and prevent them, and thus torment your body and your mind. When you torment your body, then you feel suffering in your body; when you torment your mind, then you feel suffering in your mind. And that is why I say that nirvana is mixed with suffering."

"What you call suffering, Great King, is not what we call nirvana; it is the preliminary to nirvana, the search for nirvana. Nirvana is all bliss and is not mixed with suffering. And I will tell you why. Is there what we might call a bliss of sovereignty which kings enjoy?"

"Indeed, venerable one, there is a bliss of sovereignty."

"But the borders become disturbed, and a king must put down the revolt; and he surrounds himself with advisors and soldiers and goes sojourning abroad. He runs about over the rough ground and is oppressed by flies and mosquitoes and wind and heat; he fights great battles and is in doubt of his very life."

"But, venerable one, that is not what we call the bliss of sovereignty; it is but a preliminary in search thereof. The king seeks for power with suffering, and then he can enjoy the bliss he has sought. The bliss of sovereignty is not mixed with suffering: the bliss is one thing and the suffering another."

"Even so, Great King, nirvana is all bliss and is not mixed with suffering. Those who seek nirvana torment their bodies and their minds: they restrain their standing and walking and sitting and eating; they interrupt their sleep; they oppress their senses; they sacrifice their bodies and their lives.

"They seek for nirvana with suffering, and then they can enjoy the bliss they have sought, even as a king enjoys the bliss of sovereignty when he has destroyed his enemies. Nirvana is all bliss and is not mixed with suffering; the bliss is one thing and the suffering another.

"And I will tell you another reason. Is there what we might call a bliss of learning which is enjoyed by learned masters?"

"Indeed, venerable one, there is a bliss of learning."

"Is that bliss of learning mixed with suffering?"

"No, it is not."

"But a student torments himself with bowing down and standing up before his teacher: he fetches the water and sweeps the house; he massages and bathes his teacher's feet; and all he gets are scraps of food. He casts aside his own mind and follows the mind of another; he sleeps in discomfort and eats bad food."

Nepalese monks study the Buddha's teachings.

"But, venerable one, that is not what we call the bliss of learning; it is but a preliminary in search thereof. The student seeks for learning with suffering, and then he can enjoy the bliss he has sought. The bliss of learning is not mixed with suffering: the bliss is one thing and the suffering another."

"Even so, Great King, nirvana is all bliss and is not mixed with suffering. Those who seek nirvana torment their bodies and their minds: they restrain their standing and walking and sitting and eating; they interrupt their sleep; they oppress their senses; they sacrifice their bodies and their lives.

"They seek for nirvana with suffering, and then they can enjoy the bliss they have sought, even as a learned master enjoys the bliss of learning. Nirvana is all bliss and is not mixed with suffering; the bliss is one thing and the suffering another."

"Excellent, venerable one. Thus it is, and thus I accept it."

*   *   *   *   *   *

"Venerable one, you are always speaking of nirvana: can you give me a metaphor, or a reason, or an argument, or an inference to show me its form, or its nature, or its duration, or its size?"

"Great King, nirvana is unique and incomparable: there is neither metaphor nor reason, neither argument nor inference, which can show its form, or its nature, or its duration, or its size."

"But venerable one, nirvana is a real thing: I simply cannot accept that there is no way to make intelligible its form, or its nature, or its duration, or its size. Explain this reasonably to me."

"Very well, Great King, I shall explain it to you. Is there such a thing as the ocean?"

"Of course there is such a thing as an ocean."

"Suppose someone were to ask you how much water there is in the ocean, and how many creatures lived therein. How would you answer such a question?"

"Foolish person, I would say, you are asking me an unanswerable thing. No one should ask such a question; such a question should be put aside. Scientists have never analyzed the ocean: no one can measure the water there, nor count the creatures who live therein. That is the way I would answer the question."

"But, Great King, the ocean is a real thing: why should you give such an answer? Should you not rather count and then say: There is so much water in the ocean, and so many creatures living therein?"

"But I could not do so, venerable one. The question is impossible."

"So the ocean is a real thing, yet you cannot measure its water nor count its creatures; and in the same way nirvana is a real thing, yet there is neither metaphor nor reason, neither argument nor inference, which can show its form, or its nature, or its duration, or its size. And even if there were a man with magic powers who could measure the waters of the ocean and count its creatures: even he could not find the form, or the nature, or the duration, or the size of nirvana."

"Venerable one, let us accept that. Is there not at least some quality of nirvana which is also found elsewhere, that it may serve as a metaphor?"

"Nothing has the same form as nirvana, but we can indeed find some things to serve as metaphors for its qualities."

"Excellent, venerable one. Quickly tell me, that I may gain some insight into even one of the qualities of nirvana. Allay the fever of my heart with the cool sweet breezes of your speech."

"One quality of the lotus is found in nirvana, Great King, and two qualities of water; three qualities of medicine, and four of the ocean; five of food, and ten of space; three of the wish-granting gem, and three of red sandalwood; three of the finest butter, and five qualities of a mountain peak are found in nirvana."

"What is the one quality of the lotus which is found in nirvana?"

"The lotus is unstained by water, Great King, and nirvana is unstained by any passion."

"And the two qualities of water?"

"Water is cool, and calms fever; and nirvana is cool, and calms the fever of all the passions. Water allays the thirst of men and beasts who are weary and thirsty, parched and overcome by heat; and nirvana allays the thirst of craving for pleasure, craving for existence, and craving for wealth."

"And the three qualities of medicine?"

"Medicine is a refuge for creatures tormented by poison; and nirvana is a refuge for creatures tormented by the poison of passion. Medicine puts an end to disease, and nirvana puts an end to all suffering. Medicine is the nectar of immortality, and nirvana is the nectar of immortality."

"What are the four qualities of the ocean which are found in nirvana?"

"The ocean is empty of all corpses, and nirvana is empty of the corpses of passion. The ocean is great and limitless, and it is not filled by all the rivers that flow into it; and nirvana is great and limitless, and it is not filled by all the beings who enter it. The ocean is the abode of great creatures; and nirvana is the abode of the great Worthy Ones, the stainless, the strong, the powerful. The ocean seems to flower with the vast and various blossoms of the waves; and nirvana seems to flower with the vast and various blossoms of purity and knowledge and freedom."

"And the the qualities of space?"

"Space does not arise, nor decay, nor die, nor pass away, nor reappear; it cannot be overcome, nor stolen by thieves; it is not supported by anything; it is the path of the birds, without obstruction, infinite. And nirvana does not arise, nor decay, nor die, nor pass away, nor reappear; it cannot be overcome, nor stolen by thieves; it is not supported by anything; it is the path of the Noble Ones, without obstruction, infinite."

"And the three qualities of the wish-granting gem?"

"The wish-granting gem grants every wish, and nirvana grants every wish. The wish-granting gem causes joy, and nirvana causes joy. The wish-granting gem shines with light, and nirvana shines with light."

"And the three qualities of red sandalwood?"

"Red sandalwood is hard to find, and nirvana is hard to find. Red sandalwood has an unequaled fragrance, and nirvana has an unequaled fragrance. Red sandalwood is praised by the discriminating, and nirvana is praised by the Noble Ones."

"And the three qualities of the finest butter?"

"The finest butter is beautiful in color, and nirvana is beautiful in virtue. The finest butter is beautiful in fragrance, and nirvana is beautiful in righteousness. The finest butter is beautiful in taste, and nirvana is beautiful in experience."

"What are the five qualities of a mountain peak which are found in nirvana?"

"Nirvana is as lofty as a mountain peak and as unmoving. A mountain peak is hard to climb, and nirvana cannot be reached by the passions. No seeds can grow on a mountain peak, and no passion can grow in nirvana. A mountain peak is free of fear or favor, and nirvana is free of fear or favor."

"Excellent, venerable one. Thus it is, and thus I accept it."

* * * * * *

"Venerable one, it is said that nirvana is neither in the past, nor in the future, nor in the present; that it is not produced, nor is it unproduced, nor is it producible. Then say a man rightly practices, and realizes nirvana: does he realize something already produced, or does he produce it first and then realize it?"

"He neither realizes something already produced, Great King, nor does he produce it first and then realize it. And yet the realm of nirvana exists, that he may rightly practice, and realize it."

"Venerable one, do not explain the question by making it dark; explain it by making it open and unconcealed. Willingly heap upon me all that you have been taught, for people are bewildered and perplexed, and full of doubt. Destroy this dagger in my heart."

"The realm of nirvana exists, Great King, calm and blissful and exalted. And a man may rightly practice, and know conditioned things according to the teachings of the Buddha, and realize nirvana with his wisdom.

"Even as a student might learn an art according to the teachings of his master, a man may rightly practice, and know

A Zen temple rock garden in Kyoto, Japan, symbolizes the journey of life.

conditioned things according to the teachings of the Buddha, and realize nirvana with his wisdom.

"And how may nirvana be known? It may be known by its safety, its security, its peace, its calm, its joy, its bliss, its purity, its coolness.

"Suppose a man were being burned in a blazing scorching fire heaped high with wood. And with great effort he freed himself and escaped into the open air where there was no fire; then he would feel the great happiness.

"Even so, Great King, a man may rightly practice and by careful attention realize nirvana, the highest happiness, wherein the three-fold fires blaze no more. For these fires of passion are the fire heaped high with wood; and the man who rightly practices is the man cast into the fire; and nirvana is the open air.

"Or suppose a man had fallen into a pit filled with excrement and the corpses of snakes and dogs and men, that he was entangled in the hair of the corpses. And with great effort he freed himself and escaped into the open air where there were no corpses; then he would feel the greatest happiness.

"Even so, Great King, a man may rightly practice and by careful attention realize nirvana, the highest happiness, wherein there are no corpses of passion. For the pleasures of your senses are the corpses; and the man who rightly practices is the man fallen into the pit; and nirvana is the open air.

"Or suppose a man had been taken by his enemies, and he shivered and trembled in his fear, and his heart was confused and distressed. And with great effort he freed himself and escaped into a place of safety, firm and secure; then he would feel the greatest happiness.

"Even so, Great King, a man may rightly practice and by careful attention realize nirvana, the highest happiness, wherein there is neither fear nor terror. For the terror you feel at birth and decay and disease and death is the fear of the man among his enemies; and the man who rightly practices is the terrified man; and nirvana is the place of safety.

"Or suppose a man had fallen into a muddy swamp, all filthy and dirty and slimy. And with great effort he removed the slimy mud and went into a place which was pure and clean; then he would feel the greatest happiness.

"Even so, Great King, a man may rightly practice and by careful attention realize nirvana, the highest happiness, wherein there is no mud of passion. For your possessions and honor and fame are mud; and the man who rightly practices is the man fallen into the swamp; and nirvana is the place which is pure and clean.

"And how does this man rightly practice, and realize nirvana? He knows conditioned things as they really are; he sees in them birth, and decay, and disease, and death; he sees in them neither happiness nor joy, nor anything worth grasping, in the beginning or the middle or the end.

"Suppose a lump of iron were heated all day, and became scorching and glowing and hot; a man could find no place to grasp it, in the beginning or the middle or the end.

"Even so, Great King, he knows conditioned things as they really are; he sees in them birth, and decay, and death; he sees in them neither happiness nor joy, nor anything worth grasping, in the beginning or the middle or the end.

"And his heart grows discontented when he sees nothing worth grasping, and his body begins to sweat; for he is without refuge or protection, and he is weary of all his existences.

"Suppose a man had fallen into a great blazing mass of fire: he would be without refuge or protection, and he would weary of the flames.

"Even so, Great King, his heart grows discontented, and his body begins to sweat; for he is without refuge or protection, and he is weary of all his existences.

"And when he has seen the terror of the world, he thinks: Blazing it is, burning and blazing and full of sorrow. If I could only find something else, something calm and exalted, something passionless and peaceful; if only I could find nirvana, wherein all these conditioned things come to rest, where clinging to rebirth is given up, where craving is destroyed.

"And his heart leaps forward from the world, and he finds peace. For he is happy, and rejoices: I have gained my freedom from the world.

"Suppose a man had chanced into a strange land and lost his way. And when he found the way out his heart would leap forward; he would be happy, and rejoice: I have found the way out at last.

"Even so, Great King, his heart leaps forward from the world, and he finds peace. For he is happy, and rejoices: I have found the way out at last.

"And he pursues that path, and strives upon it, and practices it: his mindfulness is fixed upon the goal, and his striving is fixed upon the goal, and his joy is fixed upon the goal.

"He is forever aware of the goal; and he passes beyond the world and gains his freedom. And when he has gained his freedom from the world, Great King, then this man has rightly practiced, and has realized nirvana."

"Excellent, venerable one. Thus it is, and thus I accept it."

THE SPREAD OF
BUDDHISM

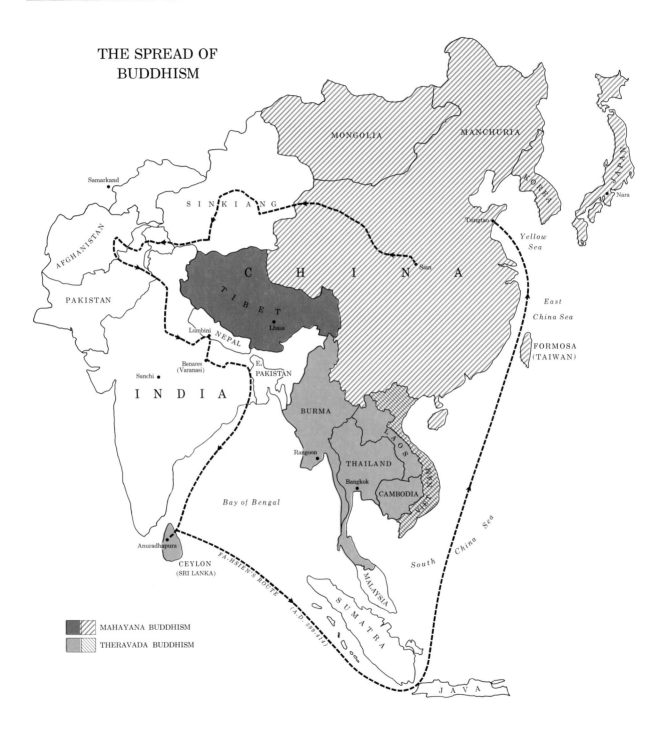

READING 8
Big Raft and Little*
HUSTON SMITH

This map shows the area over which Buddhism had spread by about A.D. 800. The area in color indicates the extent of Buddhism around the mid-twentieth century. The solid colors indicate countries that were predominantly Buddhist at that time. The hatched areas show where Buddhism is less strong. Note that Viet Nam is approximately 90 percent Mahayana and 10 percent Theravada.

Thus far we have been looking at Buddhism as it appears through its earliest records. We turn now to Buddhist history as providing one of the most fascinating evidences anywhere of the irrepressibly varied directions man's religious outreach tends to take.

When we approach Buddhist history with this interest foremost, the thing which strikes us at once is that it splits. Religions are always splitting. In our own tradition the ancient Hebrews split into Israel and Judah, Christendom into the Eastern and Western Churches, the Western Church into Roman Catholicism and Protestantism, and Protestantism has continued to splinter into its many denominations. The same happens in Buddhism. Buddha dies, and before the century is out the seeds of schism have been sown and are beginning to germinate.

One approach to the question of why Buddhism split would be through careful analysis of the events, personalities, and movements that played across the religion during its crucial early centuries. We will probably come as close to the heart of the answer, however, if we cut through all this and say simply that Buddhism divided over the questions people have always divided over.

How many such questions are there? How many questions will divide almost every human group regardless of whether it is

*Adapted from Huston Smith, *The Religions of Man* (New York: Harper & Row, 1958), pp. 117–22.

assembled in an ancient Indian village or a twentieth-century New York apartment? There seem to be at least three.

The first is the question of whether men are independent or interdependent. Some persons are most aware of themselves as individuals; the self is an independent center of freedom and initiative is to them more important than the sum of its ties. The obvious corollary is that men must, in the main, make their own ways through life; that what a man gets will be primarily of his own doing. "I was born in the slums, my father was a drunkard, every one of my brothers and sisters went to the dogs—don't talk to me about environment or influence. I got to where I am all by myself." This is one attitude. On the other side are persons to whom life seems to come in precisely the opposite mode. The separateness of their being seems scarcely real; the impressive thing is the web that binds all life together. Though our visible bodies are separate, on a deeper level, like icebergs grounded in a common floe, we are one. "Send not to ask for whom the bell tolls, it tolls for thee."

A second question concerns the relation in which man stands, not this time to his fellows, but to the universe. Is the universe friendly, on the whole helpful toward man as he reaches out for fulfillment? Or is it indifferent, perhaps even hostile to the human quest? Opinions differ. On bookstore tables one finds a book titled *Man Stands Alone* and right next to it *Man Does Not Stand Alone*. Some people see history as a venture in which man lifts himself by his own bootstraps; others are convinced that from beginning to end it is cradled in "the everlasting arms."

A third dividing question is: What is the best part of man, his head or his heart? A popular parlor pastime used to revolve around the question, "If you had to choose, would you rather be loved or respected?" It was the same point with a different twist. For some, man's crown and glory is his mind, but there are others who put his feelings higher. The first are classicists, the second romanticists; the first seek wisdom above all, the second, if they had to choose, would take compassion. The distinction probably also bears some relation to William James' contrast between the tough-minded and the tender-minded.

Here are three questions that have probably divided men since they became human and certainly continue to do so today. They divided the early Buddhists. One group said man is an individual; whatever progress he makes will be through his own doing, and wisdom above all will carry him to his goal. The other group said the opposite; man's destiny is indissolubly meshed with his fellows, grace is a fact, and love is the greatest thing in the world.

Other differences gathered around these basic ones. The first group insisted that Buddhism was a full-time job. It didn't expect everyone to make Nirvana his central goal, but those who did would have to give up the world and become monks. The second group, perhaps because it did not rest all its hopes on self-effort, was less demanding. It held that its outlook was as relevant for the layman as for the professional, that in its own way it applied as much to the world as to the monastery. This difference left its imprint on the names of the two outlooks. Each called itself a *yana,* a raft or ferry, for each proposed to carry man across the sea of life to the shore of enlightenment. The second group, however, pointing to its doctrine of grace and its ampler provisions for laymen, claimed to be the larger vehicle of the two. It preempted, accordingly, the name *Mahayana,* the Big Raft, *Maha* meaning "great" as in Mahatma (the Great Souled) Gandhi. As the name caught on, the first group came to be known by contrast as *Hinayana* or the Little Raft.

Not exactly pleased with this offensive name, the Hinayanists have preferred to speak of their brand of Buddhism as *Theravada,* or the Way of the Elders. In doing so they voice their claim to represent the original Buddhism as taught by Gautama himself. This claim is justified if we are willing to take our stand on the teachings of Buddha as recorded in the earliest texts still in existence, those of the Pali Canon, for these do lend themselves on the whole to the Theravada interpretation. But this fact has in no way discouraged the Mahayanists from their counterclaim to represent the true line of succession. They defend their claim by placing their first emphasis on Buddha's life instead of on his teachings as preserved in their earliest accounts. The conspicuous fact about his life, they assert, is that he was not concerned to slip off into Nirvana by himself but to give his life for the help of others. Because he did not dwell publicly on this motive, Theravadins, attending too narrowly to certain of his teachings, have underplayed his great renunciation and thereby missed the most essential and most vital meaning of the religion that goes by his name, for it is through his love and pity more than through his insight into the means of release from suffering that Buddhism is still alive and at work in the world. Only to a select band of intimates who he felt were capable of understanding the meanings closest to his heart did he reveal the motives that explain his life and teachings. In picking up on these, Mahayanists claim to preserve the true spirit of the Buddha and to stand in the direct line of his inspiration.

We may leave to the two schools their controversy over apostolic succession; our concern is not to judge but to understand the positions they embody. The differences that have come out thus far may be summarized by the following pairs of contrasts if we remember that they are not absolute but speak of emphases.

1. Whereas Theravada Buddhism considers man as basically an individual, his emancipation not dependent upon the salvation of others, Mahayana says the opposite. Life being one, the fate of the individual is linked with the fate of all. This, they maintain, is implicit in Buddha's cardinal doctrine of *anatta* which . . . means simply that beings and things have no ego entirely of their own. If this is so, how can we escape the corollary that "we are what we are because of what others are?" "As all other beings are sick, so I am sick." Two lines from John Whittier's "The Meeting" summarize the Mahayanist perspective on this issue.

> He findeth not who seeks his own
> The soul is lost that's saved alone.

2. Theravada holds that man is on his own in this universe. There being no superhuman gods or powers to help him over the humps, every heart should beat in accord with the iron string of self-reliance.

> By ourselves is evil done,
>   By ourselves we pain endure,
> By ourselves we cease from wrong.
>   By ourselves become we pure.
> No one saves us but ourselves,
>   No one can and no one may;
> We ourselves must tread the Path:
>   Buddhas only show the way.

For Mayahana, in contrast, grace is a fact. Peace can be at the heart of all because a boundless power, grounded in Nirvana, regards and dwells without exception in every soul, drawing each in its good time to the goal.

3. In Theravada the key virtue was *bodhi,* wisdom, with the absence of self-seeking emphasized more than the active doing of good. Mahayana moved a different word to the center: *karuna,* compassion. Unless it eventuates in compassion, wisdom is worthless. "A guard I would be to them who have no protection," runs a typical Mahayana invocation; "a guide to the voyager, a ship, a well, a spring, a bridge for the seeker of the other shore." The theme has been beautifully elaborated by Shantideva, a poet-saint . . . of Buddhism:

> May I be a balm to the sick, their healer and servitor until sickness come never again;
> May I quench with rains of food and drink the anguish of hunger and thirst;
> May I be in the famine of the age's end their drink and meat;
> May I become an unfailing store for the poor, and serve them with manifold things for their need.
> My own being and my pleasures, all my righteousness in the past, present and future, I surrender indifferently,
> That all creatures may win through to their end.[1]

4. Theravada Buddhism centers on monks. Monasteries are the spiritual focus of the lands where it predominates, reminding all of the higher truth which in the last resort gives life its meaning and is the world's final justification. Renunciation of the world is held in high national esteem, and even men who do not intend to become monks for their entire lives are expected to live as such for a year or two that their lives may take on some of the monastic virtues. Mahayana Buddhism, on the contrary, is primarily a religion for laymen. Even her priests are expected to make the service of laymen their primary concern.

5. It follows from these differences that the ideal type as projected by the two schools will also differ markedly. For the Theravadins the ideal was the *Arhat,* the perfected disciple who . . . strikes out on his own for Nirvana and with great concentration makes his way unswervingly toward that pinpointed goal. The Mahayana ideal, on the contrary, was the *Bodhisattva,* "one whose essence (*sattva*) is perfected wisdom (*bodhi*)," a being who, having brought himself to the brink of Nirvana, voluntarily

Maitreya, a Bodhisattva *("Buddha-to-be"), is mentioned in Buddhist sacred writings from the third century A.D.*

[1]From the *Bodhicharyavatara* of Shantideva.

renounces his prize that he may return to the world to make it accessible to others. He deliberately sentences himself to age-long servitude that others, drawing on his acts that go beyond what is expected, may enter Nirvana before him. The difference between the two types is illustrated in the story of four men who, journeying across an immense desert, come upon a compound surrounded with high walls. One of the four determines to find out what is inside. He scales the wall and on reaching the top gives a whoop of delight and jumps over. The second and third do likewise. When the fourth man gets to the top of the wall, he sees below him an enchanted garden with sparkling streams, pleasant groves, and delicious fruit. Though longing to jump over, he resists the impulse. Remembering other wayfarers who are trudging the burning deserts, he climbs back down and devotes himself to directing them to the oasis. The first three men were *Arhats,* the last was a *Bodhisattva,* one who vows not to desert this world "until the grass itself be enlightened."

6. This difference in ideal naturally works back to color the two schools' estimates of the Buddha himself. For one he was essentially a saint, for the other a savior. Though the Theravadins revered him as a supreme sage who set an incomparable example, he remained for them a man among men. Upon entering Nirvana his personal influence ceased; he knows nothing any more of this world of becoming, and is at perfect peace. The reverence felt by the Mahayanists could not be satisfied with such ordinary humanness. For them, Buddha is a world savior who continues to draw all creatures toward him "by the rays of his jewel hands." The bound, the shackled, the suffering on every plane of existence, galaxy beyond galaxy, worlds beyond worlds, coming into being out of the timeless void then bursting like bubbles; all are the recipients of the inexhaustible "gift rays" of the Lord Who Looks Down in Pity.

These differences are the central ones, but several others may be named to complete the picture. Whereas the Theravadins followed their founder in looking upon speculation as a useless distraction, Mahayana spawned an elaborate cosmology replete with innumerable heavens, hells, and descriptions of Nirvana. The only kind of prayer the Theravadins countenanced was meditation, whereas the Mahayanists added supplication, petition, and calling upon the name of the Buddha. Finally, whereas

Theravada remained conservative to the point of an almost fundamentalistic adherence to the early Pali texts, Mahayana was liberal in almost every respect. It accepted later texts as equally authoritative, was less strict in interpreting disciplinary rules, and held a higher regard for the spiritual possibilities of women and less gifted monks as well as laymen generally.

Covered rafts carry participants in a rice festival.

READING 9
The Image of the Crossing*
HUSTON SMITH

We have looked at different angles within Buddhism: the Little Raft and the Big Raft. . . . These angles are so different that we must ask in closing whether, on any grounds other than historical accident, they deserve to be considered aspects of a single religion.

There are two respects in which the various branches of Buddhism must be regarded as variations within a single religion. They all root back to a single founder from whom they claim to derive their teachings. Beyond this, they can all be subsumed . . . within a metaphor, a single image. This . . . is the image of the crossing, the simple everyday experience of crossing a river on a ferryboat.

To appreciate the force of this image we must remember the indispensable role the ferry plays in Eastern life. In lands laced with unbridged rivers and canals, almost any journey will require a ferry. This commonplace fact underlies and inspires every school of Buddhism, as the use of the word *yana* [meaning "raft"] by all of them clearly indicates. Buddhism is a voyage across the river of life, a transport from the common-sense shore of nonenlightenment, spiritual ignorance, desire, and death, to the far-flung bank of wisdom which brings liberation from this prevailing bondage. Compared with this agreed fact, the differences within

*Abridged and adapted from H. Smith, *The Religions of Man*, pp. 136–39.

Buddhism are no more than variations in the kind of vehicle one boards or the stage one has reached on the journey.

What are these stages? While we are on the first bank it is almost the world to us. Its earth underfoot is solid and reassuring. The rewards and disappointments of its social life are vivid and compelling. The opposite shore is barely visible and has no impact on our world of affairs.

But if something prompts us to see what the other side is like we may decide to attempt the crossing. If we are of independent bent, we may decide to make it on our own. In this case we are Theravadins or Hinayanists; we shall make ourselves a little raft and push off. Most of us, however, have neither the time nor the inclination for this kind of feat. Mahayanists, we move down the bank to where a ferryboat is expected. As the group of explorers clamber aboard at the landing there is an air of excitement. Attention is focused on the distant bank, still indistinct, but the voyagers are still very much like citizens of this side of the river. The ferry pushes off and moves across the water. The bank we are leaving behind is losing its substance. The shops and streets and ant-like figures are blending together and releasing their myriad pulls upon us. Meanwhile the shore toward which we are headed is not in focus either; it seems almost as far away as it ever was. There is an interval in the crossing when the only tangible realities are the water with its treacherous currents and the boat which is stoutly but precariously contending with them. This is the moment for Buddhism's Three Vows: I take refuge in the *Buddha*— the fact that there was an explorer who made this trip and proved to us that it is possible. I take refuge in the *dharma,* the vehicle of transport, this boat to which we have committed our lives in the conviction that it is seaworthy. I take refuge in the *sangha,* the Order, the crew that is navigating this trip and in whom we have confidence. The shoreline of the world has been left behind; until we set foot on the further bank, these are the only things in which we can trust.

The further shore draws near, becomes real. The raft jolts onto the sand and we step out upon solid ground. The land which had been misty and unsubstantial as a dream is now fact. And the shore that we left behind, which was so tangible and real, is now only a slender horizontal line, a visual patch or a memory without any hold on us.

Impatient to explore our new surroundings, we nevertheless

remember our gratitude for the splendid ship and crew who have brought us safely to what promises to be a fascinating land. It will be no act of gratitude, however, to insist on packing the boat with us as we plunge into the woods. "Would he be a clever man," Buddha asks, "if out of gratitude for the raft that has carried him across the stream to safety he, having reached the other shore, should cling to it, take it on his back, and walk about with the weight of it? Would not the clever man be the one who left the raft (of no use to him any longer) to the current of the stream, and walked ahead without turning back to look at it? Is it not simply a tool to be cast away and forsaken once it has served the purpose for which it was made? In the same way the vehicle of the doctrine is to be cast away and forsaken once the other shore of Enlightenment has been attained."[1]

. . . The rules of Buddhism, the Eightfold Path; the technical terminology of *dukkha, karuna,* Nirvana, and the rest; the sacred Order; the person of Buddha himself—all are vitally important to the individual in the act of making the crossing. They lose their relevance for those who have arrived. Indeed, if the traveler not merely reaches the shore of this promised land but keeps moving into its interior, there comes a time when not only the raft but the river itself drops out of view. When such a one turns around to look for the land that has been left behind, what does he see? What *can* one see who has crossed a horizon line beyond which the river dividing this shore from that has faded? He looks—and there is no "other shore"; there is no torrential separating river; there is no raft; there is no ferryman. These things are no longer a part of his world.

Before the river has been crossed, the two shores, human and divine, can appear only distinct from each other, different as life and death, as day and night. But once the crossing has been made and left behind, no such distinction remains. The realm of the gods is no distant place; it is where the traveler stands, and if his stance be still in this world, that world has become perfected. In this sense we are to read Buddhist assertions that "this our worldly life is an activity of Nirvana itself, not the slightest distinction exists between them."[2] . . . Having stepped out of the

[1]*Majjhima-Nikaya,* 3.2.22.135. Quoted in Heinrich Zimmer, *The Philosophies of India* (New York: Pantheon Books, 1951), pp. 477–78.
[2]Cf. Edward Conze, *Buddhism: Its Essence and Development* (New York: Philosophical Library, no date), p. 136.

delusions of his former self-assertive, self-defensive ego, he loses the separation between acceptance and rejection as well. Every moment becomes accepted completely. Like a net of perfect jewels each of which gathers into itself and throws back to the viewer the living splendor of all, every experience becomes a reflex of a power that endures, untouched by pain. From such a perspective the tragic view of life becomes Byronic, adolescent, and self-conscious. Even the categories of good and evil are thrown back into solution. "That which is sin is also Wisdom," we read; "the realm of Becoming is also Nirvana."[3]

From this new shore we are in a position to understand the profound intuition that underlies the *Bodhisattva's* vow of renunciation. He has paused on the brink of Nirvana, resolved to forego entering the untroubled pool of eternity "until the grass itself be enlightened," which, as grass keeps coming, means until the end of time. Does this mean that he may never, himself, reach total fulfillment? It means, rather, that he has risen to the point where the distinction between time and eternity has lost its force, having been made by the rational mind but dissolved in the perfect knowledge of the lightning-and-thunder insight that has transcended the pairs of opposites. Time and eternity are now two aspects of the same experience-whole, two sides of the same unsliceable completeness. "The jewel of eternity is in the lotus of birth and death."

From the standpoint of normal, worldly consciousness there must always remain a baffling inconsistency between this climactic insight and worldly prudence. But the world will always look different to those who have not been portered across the ocean of ignorance and to those who have. Only the latter can see through the delusory distinctions between time and eternity. The river separating the two shores has faded from view. Or if to one with eagle vision it still remains, it is seen now as connecting the two banks. . . .

[3]Ramprasad. Quoted in H. Zimmer, op cit., p. 602.

READING 10
What the Buddha Taught and the World Today*
WALPOLA SRI RAHULA

A Nepalese woman, seated by her spinning, holds a prayer wheel and fingers her prayer beads.

There are some who believe that Buddhism is so lofty and sublime a system that it cannot be practised by ordinary men and women in this workaday world of ours, and that one has to retire from it to a monastery, or to some quiet place, if one desires to be a true Buddhist.

This is a sad misconception, due evidently to a lack of understanding of the teaching of the Buddha. People run to such hasty and wrong conclusions as a result of their hearing, or reading casually, something about Buddhism written by someone, who, as he has not understood the subject in all its aspects, gives only a partial and lopsided view of it. The Buddha's teaching is meant not only for monks in monasteries, but also for ordinary men and women living at home with their families. The Noble Eightfold Path, which is the Buddhist way of life, is meant for all, without distinction of any kind.

The vast majority of people in the world cannot turn monk, or retire into caves or forests. However noble and pure Buddhism may be, it would be useless to the masses of mankind if they could not follow it in their daily life in the world of today. But if you understand the spirit of Buddhism correctly, . . . you can surely follow and practise it while living the life of an ordinary man.

There may be some who find it easier and more convenient to

*From Rahula, *What the Buddha Taught,* rev. ed., pp. 76–78, 80–81.

accept Buddhism, if they do live in a remote place, cut off from the society of others. Others may find that that kind of retirement dulls and depresses their whole being both physically and mentally, and that it may not therefore be conducive to the development of their spiritual and intellectual life.

True renunciation does not mean running away physically from the world. Sariputta, the chief disciple of the Buddha, said that one man might live in a forest devoting himself to ascetic practices, but might be full of impure thoughts . . .; another might live in a village or a town, practising no ascetic discipline, but his mind might be pure. . . . Of these two, said Sariputta, the one who lives a pure life in the village or town is definitely far superior to, and greater than, the one who lives in the forest.

The common belief that to follow the Buddha's teaching one has to retire from life is a misconception. It is really an unconscious defence against practising it. There are numerous references in Buddhist literature to men and women living ordinary, normal family lives who successfully practised what the Buddha taught, and realized Nirvana. Vacchagotta the Wanderer . . . once asked the Buddha straightforwardly whether there were laymen and women leading the family life, who followed his teaching successfully and attained to high spiritual states. The Buddha categorically stated that there were not one or two, not a hundred or two hundred or five hundred, but many more laymen and women leading the family life who followed his teaching successfully and attained to high spiritual states. . . .

One might now ask: If a man can follow Buddhism while living the life of an ordinary layman, why was the Sangha, the Order of monks, established by the Buddha? The Order provides opportunity for those who are willing to devote their lives not only to their own spiritual and intellectual development, but also to the service of others. An ordinary layman with a family cannot be expected to devote his whole life to the service of others, whereas a monk, who has no family responsibilities or any other worldly ties, is in a position to devote his whole life 'for the good of the many, for the happiness of the many' according to the Buddha's advice. That is how in the course of history, the Buddhist monastery became not only a spiritual centre, but also a centre of learning and culture. . . .

If one desires to become a Buddhist, there is no initiation ceremony (or baptism) which one has to undergo. (But to become a *bhikkhu,* a member of the Order of the *Sangha,* one has to undergo a long process of disciplinary training and education.) If one understands the Buddha's teaching, and if one is convinced that his teaching is the right Path and if one tries to follow it, then one is a Buddhist. But according to the unbroken age-old tradition in Buddhist countries, one is considered a Buddhist if one takes the Buddha, the *Dhamma* (the Teaching) and the *Sangha* (the Order of Monks)—generally called 'the Triple-Gem'—as one's refuges, and undertakes to observe the Five Precepts—the minimum moral obligations of a lay Buddhist—(1) not to destroy life, (2) not to steal, (3) not to commit adultery, (4) not to tell lies, (5) not to take intoxicating drinks—reciting the formulas given in the ancient texts. On religious occasions Buddhists in congregation usually recite these formulas, following the lead of a Buddhist monk.

There are no external rites or ceremonies which a Buddhist has to perform. Buddhism is a way of life, and what is essential is following the Noble Eightfold Path. Of course there are in all Buddhist countries simple and beautiful ceremonies on religious occasions.

A monk turns the prayer wheels at the Swayambhunath Temple near Kathmandu, Nepal.

READING 11
The Morals of the Monk*

The following extract is part of a long composition in praise of the Buddha, leading up to a description of his perfect wisdom. The moral virtues attributed to him in the earlier part of the passage, which is quoted here, are those after which every monk should strive; and, allowing for their different circumstances, the monk's example should be followed as far as possible by the layman.

[From *Digha Nikaya,* 1.4 ff.]

The monk Gautama has given up injury to life, he has lost all inclination to it; he has laid aside the cudgel [club] and the sword, and he lives modestly, full of mercy, desiring in compassion the welfare of all things living.

He has given up taking what is not given, he has lost all inclination to it. He accepts what is given to him and waits for it to be given; and he lives in honesty and purity of heart. . . .

He has given up unchastity, he has lost all inclination to it. He is celibate and aloof, and has lost all desire for sexual intercourse, which is vulgar. . . .

He has given up false speech, he has lost all inclination to it. He speaks the truth, he keeps faith, he is faithful and trustworthy, he does not break his word to the world. . . .

He has given up slander, he has lost all inclination to it. When he hears something in one place he will not repeat it in another in

*Adapted from Wm. Theodore de Bary, gen. ed., *Sources of Indian Tradition*, Vol. I (New York: Columbia University Press, 1958), pp. 114–15.

order to cause strife, . . . but he unites those who are divided by strife, and encourages those who are friends. His pleasure is in peace, he loves peace and delights in it, and when he speaks he speaks words which make for peace. . . .

He has given up harsh speech, he has lost all inclination to it. He speaks only words that are harmless, pleasing to the ear, touching the heart, cultured, pleasing the people, loved by the people. . . .

He has given up frivolous talk, he has lost all inclination to it. He speaks at the right time, in accordance with the facts, with words full of meaning. His speech is memorable, timely, well illustrated, measured, and to the point.

He does no harm to seeds or plants. He takes only one meal a day, not eating at night, or at the wrong time [that is, after midday]. He will not watch shows, or attend fairs with song, dance, and music. He will not wear ornaments, or adorn himself with garlands, scents, or cosmetics. He will not use a high or large bed. He will not accept gold or silver, raw grain or raw meat. He will not accept women or girls, bondmen or bondwomen, sheep or goats, fowls or pigs, elephants or cattle, horses or mares, fields or houses. He will not act as go-between or messenger. He will not buy or sell, or falsify with scales, weights, or measures. He is never crooked, will never bribe, or cheat, or defraud. He will not injure, kill, or put in bonds, or steal, or do acts of violence.

READING 12
Duties of the Lay Followers*

This selection, from the Vyaggahapajja *and the* Sigalovada Sutta, *gives the Buddha's instructions to the laymen.*

Four requisites for earning wealth: dauntless energy in wealth, mindfulness in keeping what is earned, simple living, and keeping company with good people.

Four bad actions to be avoided: killing, stealing, unlawful sexual indulgence, and falsehood.

Four ways of doing injustice to be avoided: doing injustice due to partiality, or due to hatred, or due to fear, or due to ignorance (that is, through deception).

Six things leading to loss of wealth which are to be avoided: addiction to drinking liquor, to walking in the streets at untimely hours, to visiting feasts, to gambling, to bad companions, or to laziness.

Ministry to parents: a child should minister to his parents by supporting them, doing his duties, continuing the family line, acting in such a way as to be worthy of his inheritance, and offering alms in honor of the departed parents.

Ministry of parents to their children: restraining them from the bad, exhorting them to do good, giving them a good education,

*From Lucien Stryk, ed., *World of the Buddha: A Reader* (New York: Doubleday & Co., Anchor Books, 1968), pp. 236–37.

arranging a suitable marriage in due time, handing over the inheritance to them at the proper time.

Ministry of students to teachers: rising before the teacher, attending to the needs of the teacher, listening attentively, doing personal service to the teacher, and carefully receiving instruction.

Ministry of teachers to students: giving the students the best training, showing them how to grasp things well, teaching them suitable arts and science, introducing them to their friends and companions, keeping them safe in every way.

Ministry of husband to wife: honoring her, avoiding disrespect, being faithful to her, entrusting his treasure to her custody, providing her with garments and ornaments.

Ministry of wife to husband: doing her duties in perfect order, treating the friends and relatives of her husband generously and hospitably, being faithful to him, protecting carefully the treasure entrusted to her, and doing all her duties diligently.

Ministry to friends and companions: showing generosity, speaking courteously, prompting good, treating them with equality, and being truthful to them.

Ministry of friends and companions in return: looking after him when he is careless, safeguarding his property when he is negligent, rendering assistance when he is in trouble, and protecting his children and advancing their welfare.

Ministry to servants and employees: apportioning work to them according to their strength, providing them with food and wages, tending them in sickness, sharing special dainties with them, and giving them rest and holidays at the proper times.

Ministry of servants and employees to their master: rising before him, going to sleep after him, taking only what is given, carrying out his orders promptly and with pleasure, and giving him a good report.

Ministry to members of the Sangha: speaking to them with affection, showing friendliness in deed, thinking of them respectfully, being generous in supplying their wants readily, providing them with their material needs.

Ministry of members of the Sangha to a lay devotee: dissuading him from evil, exhorting him to the good, loving him with a kind heart, teaching him what he has not heard and making clear what he has already heard, pointing out to him the path to a happy state.

These kindergarten children in Kyoto are being taught the Buddhist love for all creatures on earth.

Glossary

Definitions are limited to those that apply to usage of words and phrases within this book. Italic words in the definitions are defined elsewhere in the Glossary.

Ananda. *Gautama Buddha*'s cousin and disciple who, according to some sources, persuaded the *Buddha* to allow women to become nuns.

Anatta (also spelled *anatman*). The doctrine that there is no permanent self or soul, but only a complex of mental and physical elements that succeed one another continuously and can be disciplined to attain Nirvana.

Apostolic succession. In Christianity, the uninterrupted succession from the Apostles. In Buddhism, the controversy between the *Theravadins* and the *Mahayanists* as to which group is in direct line to the *Buddha*'s inspiration.

Arhat (also spelled *arahant, arhant*). One who has achieved *enlightenment* and eliminated *samsara;* among the *Theravadins*, the ideal disciple who unswervingly makes his way toward Nirvana.

Aryans. People of Iran and India who spoke an Indo-European language.

Ascetic. One who practices *asceticism*.

Asceticism. The exercise of extreme austerity and self-denial for purposes of purification and sanctification.

Asoka. Emperor of India in the third century B.C. He became a Buddhist and started an extensive missionary movement to spread Buddhism.

Baptism. In Christianity, a sacrament of admission into the membership of the church.

Bhikkhu. A member of the Buddhist monastic order of the *Sangha*.

Big Raft. A term used by *Mahayanists* referring to the symbolism of the Mahayanists.

Bodhi. *Enlightenment* or wisdom; the tree (also called bo tree) under which the *Buddha* sat for forty-nine days undergoing an inner struggle to find truth.

Bodhisattva. Among the *Mahayanists,* the ideal disciple who voluntarily renounces Nirvana in order to return to the world and help others attain it.

Brahma. The creator-god in *Hinduism.* At the time of the *Buddha,* Brahma was looked on as the high god in parts of India.

Brahman. In *Hinduism,* the impersonal spirit of the universe or the "reality" which the universe reflects. Also used to refer to priestly caste.

Brahmanism. The religion of the *Brahmins* and Hindus.

Brahminical. Of or relating to the Brahmin caste of India.

Brahmins (also spelled *Brahmans*). In *Hinduism,* the highest *caste*—that of priest-scholars.

Buddha. One who has achieved complete *enlightenment.*

Buddha, The. Siddhartha *Gautama,* the founder of Buddhism.

Caste. A hereditary social system of India in which members must follow severe restrictions and rules in matters such as occupations, marriage, social contact, and everyday activities such as eating and drinking.

Confucianism. The teachings of *Confucius,* which emphasize moral and ethical behavior.

Confucius. A Chinese philosopher born in the sixth century B.C. whose teachings formed the basis for *Confucianism.*

Dhamma. The Pali spelling of *dharma.*

Dharma. Duty, essential nature; in Buddhism, the *Buddha*'s teachings or doctrine; the ideal truth.

Dhyana. A state of mental concentration (meditation) during which the individual passes through four stages, from repudiation of passions and doubt to pure serenity and absence of sensation.

Digha Nikaya. The first section of the *Pali Canon;* contains long dialogues dealing with the *Buddha*'s teachings.

Dukkha. Suffering; thirst, desire, or passion; first of Four Noble Truths.

Eastern (Orthodox) churches. Christian churches in the eastern half of the Roman Empire which broke with Rome and which follow a distinctly Eastern rite of worship.

Enlightenment. A state in which the individual achieves Universal Truth and is no longer subject to human needs or pain; the elimination of *samsara;* Nirvana.

Five Precepts, The. The obligations of a lay Buddhist to refrain from killing, stealing, committing adultery, lying, and becoming intoxicated.

Four Passing Sights, The. The child *Gautama*'s witnessing of old age, sickness, death, and a wandering *ascetic* that led him to renounce the world and become a *monk.*

Gandhi, Mohandas K. ("Mahatma"). A Hindu nationalist leader who, through nonviolent resistance to British occupation, helped bring about India's independence in 1947.

Gautama Buddha (Siddhartha). The founder of Buddhism, born in what is now Nepal around 560 B.C. and died around 480 B.C.

Hair shirt. Cloth made of animal hair worn next to the skin as a form of penance.

Hebrews. A northern Semitic people to whom the ancient Israelites belonged.

Hermit. One who renounces the world and lives apart from society in order to achieve sanctification or religious perfection; a recluse.

Hinayana. The *Little Raft,* or Smaller or Lesser Vehicle (terms coined and used by *Mahayanists*). See *Theravada Buddhism.* Hinayana also refers to the *Buddha*'s teachings as found in the *Pali Canon.*

Hinayanists. Another name for *Theravadins* (used by *Mahayanists*).

Hinduism. The principal religion of India consisting of numerous cults and mystical practices and emphasizing the role of *dharma* in human life.

Indo-Aryan. A tall, fair-skinned, dark-haired Indian people speaking an Indo-European language.

Islam. The religion founded by Muhammad in the early seventh century which teaches that there is but one God, Allah, and Muhammad is his Prophet.

Israel. An ancient kingdom of Palestine occupied by the *Hebrews* and later split into two kingdoms—Israel and *Judah.*

Jainism. An Indian religion founded by Mahavira in the sixth century B.C. whose central doctrines are the perfectibility of mankind and a reverence for all forms of life.

Judah. The southern kingdom of the *Hebrews* in ancient Palestine. See *Israel.*

Judaism. The religion of the Jews, characterized by a belief in one God.

Karma. An action or deed and its consequence; the concept derived from the ancient belief that what you do in this life will affect future rebirths.

Karuna. Compassion, a key virtue of a *Bodhisattva.*

Little Raft. A term used by *Mahayanists* referring to the symbolism of the *Theravadins.*

Lotus. A type of water lily often used as a religious symbol in Buddhism and *Hinduism.*

Magadha. An ancient kingdom in northeastern India comprising parts of modern-day Bihar State. This kingdom was prominent during the time of the *Buddha*.

Mahatma. An Indian title of honor given to a person held in great esteem or reverence.

Mahayana. The *Big Raft,* or Great Vehicle (terms coined and used by *Mahayanists*). See *Mahayana Buddhism.*

Mahayana Buddhism. A branch of Buddhism that teaches one should not pursue Nirvana singlemindedly, but must show love and compassion toward others in order to bring them, too, to Nirvana.

Mahayanists. Those who practice *Mahayana Buddhism.*

Majjhima Nikaya. A section of the *Pali Canon* which contains dialogues relating to the *Buddha*'s teachings.

Mantra. A verbal spell or mystical formula used in both Buddhism and *Hinduism.*

Mara. The devil, or Evil One, who tempted *Gautama Buddha.*

Milinda. An Indo-Greek king of a land comprising parts of present-day Afghanistan and West Pakistan whose "questions" to the monk *Nagasena* form the work known as the Milindapanha.

Moksha. Release from the cycle of continuous rebirth, or *samsara.*

Monastery. The religious house where *monks* live.

Monk. One who lives a communal life in a religious house and performs certain works and devotions in the service of a deity or in order to attain a religious goal. Some Buddhist monks may live solitary, wandering lives in their pursuit of Nirvana.

Nagasena. A scholarly Buddhist monk who answers King *Milinda*'s "questions" in the Milindapanha.

Noble Ones, The. Those who follow the Noble Eightfold Path.

Non-Aryans. Those who are not of *Aryan,* or Indo-European, stock.

Order, Sacred. See *Sangha.*

Pali. The language of *Theravadins.*

Pali Canon. The earliest-known *scriptures* of Buddhism, written in the *Pali* language around the first century B.C.

Passing Sights. See *Four Passing Sights, The.*

Precepts, The Five. See *Five Precepts, The.*

Pyre. The structure on which a dead body is burned in a funeral rite.

Raft. See *Big Raft* and *Little Raft.*

Rahula. Siddhartha *Gautama*'s son.

Rajagaha. Capital of the ancient kingdom of *Magadha.*

Recluse. See *Hermit.*

Rite. A prescribed ceremony.

Sakya. The clan into which Siddhartha *Gautama* was born.

Sakyamuni. A sage or teacher of the *Sakya* clan; another name for *Gautama Buddha.*

Samsara. The Hindu concept of a world of constant activity and continual rebirth, symbolized by a circle of life with no beginning and no end. Buddhism as well as *Hinduism* seeks to break this circle.

Sangha. A monastic order founded by *Gautama Buddha* whose members must wear yellow robes, shave their heads, use begging bowls, and practice daily meditation.

Sanskrit. The classical language of India and *Hinduism*.

Sariputta. One of the *Buddha*'s principal disciples.

Schism. A split within or a separation from a religious body.

Scriptures. The sacred writings of a religion.

Shinto. A Japanese religion consisting of numerous cults and deities in which the emperor came to be worshipped as a descendant of the sun-goddess.

Siddhartha. See *Gautama Buddha*.

Sikhism. A militant, monotheistic religion of India that originated around 1500 as a revolt against *Brahminical Hinduism*.

Skandhas. The five elements or factors that make up the individual: body, feelings, perception, predispositions, and consciousness.

Socrates. A Greek philosopher born in the fifth century B.C.

Taoism. A Chinese philosophy originating in the sixth century B.C. emphasizing peacefulness, simplicity, and naturalness.

Tathagata. "Truth-revealer," another name for *Gautama Buddha*.

Theravada Buddhism. A branch of Buddhism that teaches one should pursue Nirvana as the central goal of life, letting nothing or no one interfere with the quest.

Theravadins. Those who practice *Theravada Buddhism*.

Three Vows, The. The vows taken by members of the *Sangha;* the three things on which one must rely in making the "crossing" to Nirvana: the *Buddha* (the explorer who has gone before), the *dharma* (the boat), and the *Sangha* (the crew); the Triple-Gem.

Transmigration. The passage of the soul into another body at death; the cycle of rebirth.

Triple-Gem. See *Three Vows, The*.

Ultimate Reality. The highest wisdom, which one achieves only when the mind is rendered totally pure through meditation.

Upanishads. The final section of the Indian Vedic *scriptures*, which detail Hindu beliefs about the universe and *Ultimate Reality*.

Vaishya. In the Indian caste system, the merchant or agricultural class, which ranks below the *Brahmins* and warriors and above the artisans.

Way of the Elders. Another name for *Theravada Buddhism*.

Worthy Ones, The. Those who have attained Nirvana.

Yana. Raft or ferryboat.

Yasodhara. Siddhartha *Gautama*'s wife.

Yoga. A branch of *Hinduism* that subscribes to the raja-yoga as a means of self-realization; a system of exercises designed to bring about mental and physical well-being.

Zoroastrianism. A Persian religion originating in the sixth century B.C. whose followers worshipped Ahura Mazda, the god of kindness and light.